Enabling Excellence

To JENNY FOSTER,

A VERY SPECIAL COLLEAGUE
AND FRIEND FROM MY
NIKE YEARS WHO ALWAYS
GAVE ME GREAT SUPPORT
AND ADVICE.

MY BEST REGARDS,

Tim Pine

Also available from ASQ Quality Press:

Making Change Work: Practical Tools for Overcoming Human Resistance to Change
Brien Palmer

Lean Kaizen: A Simplified Approach to Process Improvements
George Alukal and Anthony Manos

The Quality Improvement Handbook, Second Edition
ASQ Quality Management Division; John E. Bauer, Grace L. Duffy, and Russell T. Westcott, editors

Leadership For Results: Removing Barriers to Success for People, Projects, and Processes
Tom Barker

Avoiding the Corporate Death Spiral: Recognizing and Eliminating the Signs of Decline
Gregg Stocker

The Executive Guide to Improvement and Change
G. Dennis Beecroft, Grace L. Duffy, John W. Moran

Root Cause Analysis: Simplified Tools and Techniques, Second Edition
Bjørn Andersen and Tom Fagerhaug

The Magic of Self-Directed Work Teams: A Case Study in Courage and Culture Change
Paul C. Palmes

Quality management — Guidelines for realizing financial and economic benefits
ANSI/ISO/ASQ Q10014-2006

Effective Writing for the Quality Professional: Creating Useful Letters, Reports, and Procedures
Jane Campanizzi

The Quality Toolbox, Second Edition
Nancy R. Tague

To request a complimentary catalog of ASQ Quality Press publications, call 800-248-1946, or visit our Web site at http://qualitypress.asq.org.

Enabling Excellence

The Seven Elements Essential to Achieving Competitive Advantage

Timothy A. Pine

ASQ Quality Press
Milwaukee, Wisconsin

American Society for Quality, Quality Press, Milwaukee 53203
© 2007 by American Society for Quality
All rights reserved. Published 2007
Printed in the United States of America
12 11 10 09 08 07   5 4 3 2 1

Library of Congress Cataloging-in-Publication Data

Pine, Timothy A., 1949–
    Enabling excellence : the seven elements essential to achieving
competitive advantage / Timothy A. Pine.
        p. cm.
    ISBN-13: 978-0-87389-714-3 (hard cover : alk. paper)
    1. Organizational effectiveness.   2. Excellence.   3. Quality control.
    4. Management.   I. Title.
    HD58.9.P56   2007
    658.3'124—dc22

                                                    2007002924

Publisher: William A. Tony
Acquisitions Editor: Matt Meinholz
Project Editor: Paul O'Mara
Production Administrator: Randall Benson

ASQ Mission: The American Society for Quality advances individual, organizational, and community excellence worldwide through learning, quality improvement, and knowledge exchange.

Attention Bookstores, Wholesalers, Schools, and Corporations: ASQ Quality
Press books, videotapes, audiotapes, and software are available at quantity
discounts with bulk purchases for business, educational, or instructional use. For
information, please contact ASQ Quality Press at 800-248-1946, or write to ASQ
Quality Press, P.O. Box 3005, Milwaukee, WI 53201-3005.

To place orders or to request a free copy of the ASQ Quality Press Publications
Catalog, including ASQ membership information, call 800-248-1946. Visit our
Web site at www.asq.org or http://qualitypress.asq.org.

Quality Press
600 N. Plankinton Avenue
Milwaukee, Wisconsin 53203
Call toll free 800-248-1946
Fax 414-272-1734
www.asq.org
http://www.asq.org/quality-press
http://standardsgroup.asq.org
E-mail: authors@asq.org

∞ Printed on acid-free paper

*To Karl Wojahn—leader, humanitarian,
motivator, friend, and mentor par excellence!*

Contents

List of Figures

Preface

I love the expression, "There is never enough time for everything, but there is plenty of time for focus." With today's growing pressures to achieve higher quality and productivity with fewer resources, there is no time for getting bogged down, sidetracked, and frustrated with clutter, trivia, or minutiae. To really succeed in today's competitive environment, one must constantly stay focused on what is truly vital. The key, of course, is identifying and isolating the vital from the trivial.

Over the past few decades, I've observed organizations underutilizing their limited and precious resources on nonvital activities. The return on their invested resources (the effectiveness of these organizations) was inferior to the best-in-class organizations and put them at a significant competitive disadvantage. They either had the wrong focus or they had no focus at all. They needed a new plan. They needed a new strategy, one focused on the vital elements that enable excellence in quality, productivity, and organizational effectiveness.

These observations inspired me to identify and isolate the important characteristics and causes for the success of the best-in-class organizations. I then concentrated these success characteristics and causes into seven vital elements. *Enabling Excellence: The Seven Elements Essential to Achieving Competitive Advantage* will provide any organization with an important and sound foundation for a quality excellence philosophy and strategic plan.

The concepts and principles of this book are universal and can be applied to any and all jobs and industries where organizational effectiveness and competitive advantage are desired. This book should especially be read by management personnel with the authority and resources to implement change.

During the process of planning and writing this book, an important objective was the efficient communication of vital information. Keeping in mind the famous Albert Einstein quote, "If you can't explain it simply, you don't understand it well enough," I attempted to make *Enabling Excellence* easy to read, concise, and clear, with just a touch of humor. Many pictures and photos have been used throughout the book to help describe and clarify concepts. They may also help facilitate and improve the reader's recall of the vital elements and concepts presented.

My sincere hope and prayer is that this book will help guide and inspire individuals and organizations toward higher levels of effectiveness and competitiveness.

Acknowledgments

Now, our God, we give you thanks,
and praise your glorious name.

1 Chronicles 29:13 (NIV)

A nice benefit of writing this book is having a unique opportunity to formally and publicly express appreciation, gratitude, and love to some very special people who have been a major positive influence in my life.

First, to the person who has been the greatest inspiration in my life, who is the epitome of personal excellence in life, who gives unconditional love, kindness, and generosity to all she comes in contact with, who lives a principle-centered life based on a rock-solid faith, and who has such uncommon modesty and humility that these sentiments and truths will undoubtedly cause her some embarrassment. My first and eternal gratitude goes to my darling mother, Phyllis Pine.

I am very fortunate to have had many mentors in my career, and I am truly grateful for each one. There are two, however, who stand out because of the huge impact they have had, not just on my career, but also on my life.

The first is Karl Wojahn, a retired toy industry executive (Mattel, Arco, Kenner Parker) who hired me right out of college and began tirelessly teaching, challenging, inspiring, and guiding me for the first 17 years of my career, as I grew from engineer to vice president. His mentoring, guidance, and friendship continues today. In fact, this book exists today because of his persistent encouragement for me to write it.

The second is Joe Fortino, retired president of several Sara Lee divisions and a former toy executive (Fisher-Price, Tonka Kenner Parker, Tyco, and Mattel) for whom I had the pleasure and privilege of working. His leadership, work ethic, integrity, and passion for excellence inspired his organizations to innovate and achieve record-breaking levels of performance.

Today, multitudes from Joe Fortino's past organizations continue to rely on his lessons and examples to guide their companies to higher levels of performance.

Keki Bhote, quality guru and author extraordinaire, has greatly inspired me with his many outstanding books on quality management. He brings together such powerful content, superb clarity, and interesting style to create works that are true masterpieces.

Tim Schuh, a highly respected and trusted associate, provided valuable reviews and constructive comments on early drafts. I am very grateful for his support and friendship.

Finally, my deepest gratitude goes to my family for their unconditional love and support:

My sister, Jan Nordstrom, whose opinions and viewpoints I highly respect and value and who provided critical reviews and excellent suggestions on the first drafts.

My brother, Roger Pine, whom I have always regarded as the consummate gentleman of the highest integrity.

My daughter, Julie Pine, whose extraordinary courage, optimism, and adventurous spirit I greatly respect and admire.

My son, Steven Pine, whose pure kindness, brilliance, and wonderful sense of humor I greatly admire and respect.

And above all, my beautiful wife Pat, whose values, insights, strength, and support have had such a positive impact on my life. She is the love of my life and I am a far better man because of her.

Timothy A. Pine
January 2007

1

Introduction

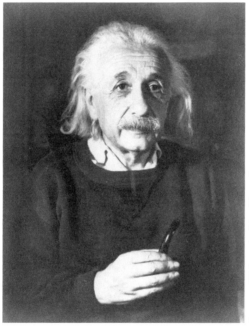

If you can't explain it simply,
you don't understand it well enough.

—*Albert Einstein*

CUT THROUGH THE CLUTTER AND FOCUS

There is such a plethora of information out there on quality excellence that it can be quite overwhelming for the person who is just looking for simple, effective guidance. The great number of books, articles, and speeches describing a wide range of techniques, practices, and opinions actually adds more complexity and confusion than clarity.

Clearly, there is just not enough time for everything, but there is plenty of time for focus. The aim of this book is to reduce and simplify into a vital few basic elements the foundation that will enable excellence and competitive advantage. It is also intended to provide guidance and reference for strategic and business planning to improve effectiveness, efficiency, and consumer loyalty.

STATE OF THE ART VS. PERFECTION

Achieving excellence in a product or service means achieving state-of-the-art quality, safety, and value as experienced and perceived by the consumer of that product or service. Achieving excellence does not mean achieving perfection. Just as there is no such thing as a perfectly safe product, there is no such thing as a perfect product or service. It can always be better. Therefore, the goal is to always be at the state-of-the-art standard with your product or service. When the right strategy is applied, this goal of product or service excellence can be readily achieved with certainty.

COMPREHENSION VS. COMMITMENT

It is interesting that new management programs often arrive with lots of fanfare, slogans, and management exhortations. When this happens, it appears that management's primary objective is to motivate and inspire the organization rather than to provide new tools for easier, more effective job performance. It ends up looking like a motivation program that is expected to increase everyone's commitment to quality, efficiency, and productivity. Evidently this "increased commitment" is supposed to drive folks to increase their efforts and work harder.

Achieving excellence, however, is not about commitment! Most organizations are already committed to excellence. If it were only about commitment, then just about everyone would already be achieving excellence in product and service. People don't need to work harder; they need to work smarter.

Achieving excellence is about comprehension. It is about understanding what to do and how to do it. It is about educating the organization to understand and apply the right tools and processes. It is about enabling the organization with comprehension, not pushing it for more commitment.

MISTAKES VS. ERRORS

It is important to distinguish between errors and mistakes. An *error* is a defect or a failure to satisfy a specification or requirement. Errors are bad. Errors are avoidable. They can be prevented.

To make a *mistake* is to fail at something new that has not only a potentially high return but also a significant risk. Important inventions and breakthroughs occur because organizations or individuals take significant risks for the potential reward of a significant success. Thomas Edison failed thousands of times before he finally succeeded in inventing the lightbulb.

The point is that mistakes are good and errors are bad. Those who make the most mistakes win. Those who make the most errors lose.

THE FOUNDATION FOR EXCELLENCE

Over the past several decades, many new business improvement programs have appeared with much promise, enthusiasm, and anticipation. Some examples of these programs are statistical process control (SPC), total quality management (TQM), quality circles, reengineering the corporation, Six Sigma, Lean Manufacturing, and Lean Enterprise. Each of these programs, without question, offers a significant business improvement opportunity. Clearly, some businesses have realized substantial value from some or all of these programs, including improvement in productivity, quality, cost reduction, and customer service.

Many businesses, however, were disappointed and disillusioned by the relatively little improvement realized from their efforts and investment. Why the big difference? Why do some companies work so hard and struggle so much yet achieve so little improvement in their quest for excellence?

The answer is that the fundamentals are not in place to form the foundation for achieving excellence. These businesses are trying to build a complicated structure (a business improvement program) on top of an inadequate foundation. The result is a structural collapse. The program cannot be supported and, therefore, fails to deliver the anticipated results.

There are seven vital elements that make up the foundation of any excellence program. With all seven in place, a business can thrive, especially in the presence of new improvement initiatives. When even just one of the elements is missing or inadequate, success is jeopardized.

THE SEVEN VITAL ELEMENTS

The key to achieving sustainable quality excellence can be reduced to just seven necessary elements. Those seven elements, each covered in a separate chapter, are as follows:

- *Prevention*—Eliminating opportunities for error

- *Consumer focus*—Building consumer loyalty

- *Process capability*—A successful mission depends on capable processes

- *Process control*—Maintaining balance and control with precise, timely adjustments

- *Variation reduction*—Zero variation means no tolerances are needed

- *The Pareto principle*—Isolating the vital from the trivial

- *Breakthrough improvement*—Innovation for superior product and market share

Each chapter has been constructed to concisely define each element and to focus on the key topics that describe each one. The idea is to provide a simple, clear, and concise roadmap to facilitate a complete comprehension of the foundation for excellence. Incorporate these seven elements into your strategic plan and culture and you will enable product excellence. If, however, any of the seven elements are missing, then achieving sustainable product excellence will not be assured, and quality, safety, costs, and schedules will likely be compromised.

To facilitate comprehension of these seven critical elements, every attempt has been made to keep the presentations and discussions simple, brief, and relevant. In the quest for simplicity, clarity, and brevity, pictures have been used, where practical, to help describe and reinforce the concepts.

Finally, it should be emphasized that all of the concepts in this book are universal. They apply to all jobs in all industries. Throughout the book the term *error* is often used instead of *defect* because it is a more general term, applicable to all jobs, including those in finance, human resources, and sales as well as the product creation and operations areas. Also, the terms *product* and *product excellence* are commonly used, even though it is understood that the basic concepts also apply to service industries.

2
Prevention

Focus on Sport/Getty Images

It's about eliminating opportunities for error.

8   *Chapter Two*

THE PREVENTION CONCEPT

The concept of prevention is the most important of the seven elements essential for achieving excellence. In fact, each of the other six elements relates to and significantly supports the prevention concept. *Prevention* means successfully applying appropriate tools and processes to prevent the occurrence of defects, errors, and waste.

The prevention concept is really about eliminating opportunities for error. It is about eliminating costs associated with poor quality. It is about minimizing the total cost of quality.

All quality costs can be grouped into one of four quality cost categories: prevention, appraisal, internal failure, and external failure. The total cost of quality is the sum of these four cost categories. Figure 2.1 lists the major components associated with each quality cost category.

1. Prevention—*"The Good"*
   Cost of preparing for an activity so it can be performed without error. Examples:
   1.1 Strategic and business planning for quality
   1.2 Developing quality requirements and specifications
   1.3 Developing quality measurements and goals
   1.4 Education and training
   1.5 Quality orientation
   1.6 Design reviews
   1.7 Product qualification
   1.8 New supplier quality evaluations
   1.9 Supplier quality seminars
   1.10 Process capability studies
   1.11 Process control
   1.12 Preventive maintenance

Figure 2.1 Total cost of quality categories.   *(Continued)*

(Continued)

2. Appraisal—*"The Bad"*

Cost related to inspecting an output to make sure it is error-free. Examples:

2.1 Incoming, in-process, and final inspection and test

2.2 Product quality audits

2.3 Maintenance of inspection equipment

2.4 Materials and supplies for inspection

2.5 Processing and reporting on inspection data

2.6 Evaluation of stock for degradation

2.7 Status measurement and reporting

2.8 Expense account reviews

3. Internal Failure—*"The Ugly"*

Cost incurred when errors are detected before a product is delivered to the customer. Examples:

3.1 Scrap, including related labor, materials, and overhead

3.2 Rework to correct defectives

3.3 Reinspection of reworked products

3.4 100-percent sorting inspection for defectives

3.5 Engineering changes to correct a design error

3.6 Manufacturing process changes to correct deficiencies

3.7 Scrapping of obsolete product

3.8 Difference between normal selling price and reduced price due to quality

3.9 Unplanned downtime due to quality failures

3.10 Inventory shrinkage

3.11 Non-value-added activities

4. External Failure—*"The Very Ugly"*

Cost incurred when errors are not detected before a product is delivered to the customer. Examples:

4.1 Defective returns

4.2 Complaint handling

4.3 Warranty charges

Figure 2.1 (Continued)

4.4   Product recalls

4.5   Product liability lawsuits

4.6   Allowances made to customers due to substandard product

4.7   Profit margin lost due to customer defection for quality

Figure 2.1   (Continued)

The strategy must be to continually reduce the total cost of quality by investing resources in prevention. Resources are always scarce and precious, and they should not be wasted on appraisal or failure activities. A relatively small investment in prevention will yield a huge return in reduced failure costs, resulting in the desired reduction of total cost of quality.

The best organizations spend the least on quality. Let me state this again for emphasis: The best organizations spend the least on quality! They accomplish this by investing in prevention.

PLAY OFFENSE, NOT DEFENSE

Prevention is proactive. Prevention plans and prepares for an activity so it can be performed without error. It takes appropriate advance action to eliminate opportunities for error. In a real sense, prevention is about playing offense.

It may seem obvious, even intuitive, that prevention is the right approach to performing an activity. Yet, it is uncanny how rarely prevention practices are actually applied. The usual environment of great pressure for increased revenue and profit and for reduced costs, lead times, and schedules somehow drives organizations to play defense. The normal approach becomes one of proceeding immediately and prematurely with the activity and then later wasting huge amounts of time and effort on after-the-fact inspection, reworking the defectives, and taking corrective action. Ironically, the end result is often poor quality, high costs, and low profits. There didn't seem to be enough time to do the job the right way the first time, but in retrospect, there certainly was enough time to do the job over again.

Change the focus. Do not play defense! It is just too wasteful. Take the time and make the effort up front for the proper planning and preparation to eliminate opportunities for error. Do the right job the right way the first time. Go on the offense! There is no sound alternative to prevention.

PREPARE FOR ERROR-FREE PERFORMANCE

The image shown of Michael Jordan dunking a basketball is a good representation of the prevention concept. Michael Jordan is obviously a physically gifted athlete, but it was not physical talent alone that made him a great basketball player. He was also very committed to the game, but it was not his commitment alone that made the difference, either. The thing that separated him from the others was his comprehension of what must be done to succeed. It was the exceptional preparation and training that distinguished Mr. Jordan from the others. His outstanding preparation resulted in that ball going through the hoop during a critical game situation. His preparation helped to prevent errors—in this case, missed shots.

As previously stated, the term *prevention* means training, planning, and preparing so an activity can be performed without error. It means knowing and doing the right job the right way the first time. It means establishing zero errors as the quality standard. It is about eliminating opportunities for error. It is about preventing surprises. Surprises are not good! See Figure 2.2.

Figure 2.2   Preventing surprises.

THE TWO ROOT CAUSES OF MOST ERRORS

Since a key objective of achieving excellence is to eliminate defects and errors, it is instructive to look at the main causes of errors. The root cause of most errors can be classified as either lack of knowledge or lack of attention.

Lack of Knowledge

It is not the things you do know, but rather the things you don't know that can get you into trouble. The things that you *know* you don't know aren't usually a problem because you are at least aware that expert assistance is required. The things that you *don't* know you don't know are usually the big trouble-makers. Figure 2.3 shows this graphically. The point is, what you don't know doesn't have to hurt you. Chapter 8, "Break-

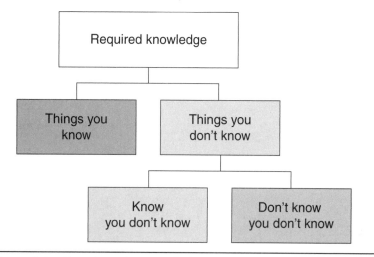

Figure 2.3   Knowing what you do know and don't know.

through Improvement," provides recommendations on how to prevent these situations from occurring.

Lack of Attention

Obviously it is impossible to be fully alert 100 percent of the time. The question is, how can we assure a complete and thorough job is being performed on critical tasks? The answer is to rely on checklists and written operating procedures.

Checklists serve as an indispensable tool to ensure the thoroughness and accuracy of important tasks. Just as a pilot uses a checklist to make sure everything is complete and correct before takeoff, a checklist can be used on most critical jobs. Of course, even though a pilot may use a checklist to ensure the equipment and flight plans are acceptable, paying attention during the flight is also important, as depicted in Figure 2.4.

Figure 2.5 provides a general checklist of hazards that can be used for ensuring a comprehensive product safety evaluation. This is an example of how checklists can help ensure thoroughness.

A process control procedure such as precontrol is another excellent tool that helps facilitate paying proper attention to a production process. Precontrol provides guidance on when to

Figure 2.4 The importance of paying attention in preventing errors.

adjust a process and when to leave it alone. When a process begins to shift or change, the precontrol procedure calls this to our attention so that proper adjustments can be made. Likewise, when a process is running properly without any special causes of variation, the precontrol procedure instructs us to leave the process alone. See Chapter 5, "Process Control," for a discussion on the precontrol tool.

ANTICIPATE AND ELIMINATE POTENTIAL FAILURES

According to U.S. Consumer Product Safety Commission injury data, approximately two-thirds of recalls and injuries (safety problems) are the result of design defects. Like safety problems, the majority of quality problems are actually designed

Mechanical	Flammability	Microbiological
Pinch point	Solids/Textiles	Bacteria/Virus
Crushing	Liquids	Yeast/Mold
Shearing	Gases	Preservative efficacy
Laceration	Mists/Dusts	Filth and contamination
Puncture		
Drop/Impact	**Thermal**	**Human factors**
Projectiles	Hot surfaces	Strength
Abrasion	Cold surfaces	Stamina
Friction	Expansion	Reaction time
Entanglement	Contraction	Human error
Entrapment	Decomposition	Stress
Stability	**Electrical**	Cognitive overload
Overload	Shock	Perception
Small parts/Choking	Overcurrent/Fires	**Control**
Aspiration	Sparks/Arcs	Inadvertent activation
Magnets/Ingestion	Batteries	Failure to activate
Strangulation		Inadequate visibility
Suction	**Toxicity**	Ambiguity
Drowning	Oral	Emergency off
	Dermal	
Falls	Inhalation	**Environment**
From elevation	Light	High temperature
Slips	Carcinogenic	Low temperature
Trips	Allergenicity	Humidity/Rain
Uneven surfaces		Ozone
Falling over	**Irritation**	Ultraviolet radiation
Falling onto	Eye	Sand/Dust
Falling with	Skin sensitization	Vacuum
	Corrosion	Lightning
Noise		Fog
Continuous	**Radiation**	
Impulsive	Ultraviolet	
	Infrared	
	Laser	

Figure 2.5   Checklist of generic hazard categories.

into the product. Design defects are especially troublesome because, unlike most manufacturing defects, they generally affect 100 percent of the units manufactured. It is therefore critical that potential hazards and failures be thoroughly identified and evaluated during the design stage of product creation. The earlier in the design stage that this evaluation occurs, the more effective and economical any issue resolution will be.

To ensure that a design is thoroughly evaluated for potential hazards, a hazard identification checklist must be used. A list of generic hazard categories that should be considered in developing a hazard identification checklist is shown in Figure 2.5. The hazard identification checklist tool should be constructed and continually upgraded as new information becomes available and new product experiences occur.

Failure modes and effects analysis (FMEA) is a commonly used procedure that examines each component of a product, considers how that component can fail, and then determines how that failure will affect the operation of the product. This procedure affords a deeper understanding of the relationships among product components and an opportunity to improve the product design by making changes to eliminate the unacceptable effects of a failure.

Building a database describing past failure modes, effects, and causes will provide a valuable tool for potential failure assessment of new designs. This type of database must be continually updated as new experiences and information become available. At a minimum, it will help prevent the recurrence of any past substandard designs.

During the early stages of design hazard and failure analysis, the risk of missing important potential hazards or failure modes can be minimized by using cross-functional teams. Teams made up of individuals from different disciplines can be especially creative, innovative, and thorough. Teams can be particularly efficient and fast at hazard and failure assessment and problem solving. It has been observed that two people working together will solve a problem in less than one-half the time it takes one person.

Prevention is being vigilant in anticipating and eliminating potential failures. This means using the hazard identification checklist, FMEA procedure, database of historical failure modes and causes, and cross-functional teamwork during the earliest stages of product creation and design.

RELY ON CERTIFICATIONS

Important elements of prevention are education, training, and communication. These are also key ingredients of any certification process. In fact, a comprehensive certification process will keep you out of the wasteful product-inspection business and make your suppliers properly assume primary ownership for quality, cost, and delivery performance.

A comprehensive certification process begins with educating your suppliers on your product, process, and systems requirements applicable to the certification. This means your requirements and specification must be clearly defined and documented. The requirements then need to be reviewed with the supplier to make sure there is a full understanding. This review may include providing some education for the supplier. It may also include follow-up testing to ensure there is sufficient knowledge and understanding.

After the education process, there should be some follow-up training to ensure the supplier is properly applying the education and achieving the desired results. Once the supplier demonstrates this, then the certification may be awarded.

The certification should be valid for a fixed period of time, perhaps one year. At the end of the certification period, a recertification should be required if both parties want to continue the business relationship.

There are different types of certification; some examples are product certification, batch certification, personnel certification, process certification, and supplier certification. The most effective certifications, however, relate to process (systems) or personnel, not to products or batches. *Remember, the process that creates the product determines product success or failure.*

Finally, it is important to perform routine supplier audits to verify continued supplier management and process performance. President Ronald Reagan said, "Trust, but verify." For our purposes here, it should be, "Educate, train, test, certify, and audit."

DEVELOP STRATEGIC PARTNERSHIPS

Most companies have a process for evaluating and approving new suppliers. Checklists are often used to ensure the prospective new supplier has adequate production capability and capacity as well as important processes and controls in place so all requirements can be satisfied. A top 10 list of questions for evaluating a potential supplier's quality capability is shown in Figure 2.6.

Probably the most important predictor of success is the attitude and behavior of the supplier's top management. If they are truly committed to completely understanding and completely satisfying all of your requirements, then the probability of success is high. Conversely, if they don't show a lot of interest or if they are reluctant to accept your requirements, the probability of success is very low.

Once you are satisfied with the supplier and begin working with them, it is important to measure and maintain metrics on the supplier's performance. At a minimum, this should include both quality (process average percent defective, total cost of quality) and delivery (on-time performance, lead-time performance). These metrics will allow you to rank each supplier based on performance so you can allocate more business to the star performers and less business to the poor performers.

All of this is fine and dandy, but what should be the real goal with respect to supplier relationships? To ensure maximum success in the twenty-first century, you must develop

1. Is top management committed to completely understanding and satisfying all of your requirements?

2. Does the supplier have adequate capability and capacity to satisfy production quantities, schedules, and product specifications?

3. Are process capability evaluations documented with adequate Cpk values?

4. Are real-time process control systems used to allow appropriate process adjustments to prevent the manufacture of nonconforming product?

5. Is there an established and practiced procedure for the evaluation, implementation, and control of product and process changes?

6. Are root causes determined and is prevention-based corrective action initiated when an unsatisfactory trend is indicated?

7. Is there a system for use, calibration, and preventive maintenance of test and production equipment?

8. Is "good housekeeping" maintained, and are clean, orderly, and secure storage facilities used to safeguard materials and product?

9. Are manufacturing processes well engineered, balanced, and lean to minimize work-in-process inventory, handling, and other non-value-added activities?

10. Is there a documented and practiced system for the selection and qualification of suppliers?

Figure 2.6 Top 10 questions for assessing supplier quality capability.

strategic partnerships with your top, key suppliers. So, what is meant by the term *strategic partnership*?

A *strategic partnership* is a commitment by both the supplier and the customer (your company) to a long-term relationship involving joint business planning and a sharing of strategies, costs, and technology. The supplier becomes an extension of your company and you ensure a stable order flow to your partner supplier. You and your partner supplier collaborate on innovations, and you provide active, concrete help to each other. It is a relationship of mutual trust, high ethics, uncompromising integrity, and transparency. A compatibility of values and a strong ethical foundation are essential criteria for selecting a partner supplier.

In a strategic partnership you need to provide your partner supplier with frequent visits, training and coaching, larger and growing volumes, much reduced competition, and higher profits and return on investment (ROI). In return, you should expect from your partner supplier a commitment to reduce and eventually terminate all work with your competition, help with the next tier of suppliers (non-partners), and a willingness to network with your other partner suppliers.

It is important to recognize that not all of your suppliers should be strategic partners. In order to guarantee a stable and growing order flow to your strategic partners, you need a base of next-tier suppliers that have a flexible (non-stable) order flow in order to accommodate your strategic partners during times of variable sales orders. By varying and reducing order allocations to these next-tier suppliers, you can maintain a stable order flow to your strategic partners.

Today, strategic partnerships will probably provide you with a significant advantage over most of your competition. Tomorrow, they most likely will be required merely to compete in the marketplace.

AVOID INSPECTION

It is very important to realize that eliminating opportunities for error is *not* accomplished with inspection. Zero errors will not be achieved by relying on inspection, even 100 percent inspection. 100 percent inspection is not 100 percent effective. Even under ideal conditions—where the defect is clearly defined and understood by the inspector; where the inspection environment is free of stress, time constraints, and distractions; and where the inspector has all of the necessary skills and tools—100 percent inspection is only about 80 percent effective.[1]

In normal, less-than-ideal conditions, 100 percent inspection can be less than 50 percent effective. This means if a lot of product that is 2 percent defective is 100 percent inspected, then the output that results could still be greater than 1 percent defective. For example, assume the lot size is 10,000 units, and within the 10,000 units there are 200 defective units (2 percent defective). If the 100 percent inspection process is only 50 percent effective, then you will only find 100 of the 200 defective units. After the 100 percent inspection and the repair of the 100 defective units, the lot of 10,000 units will still contain the other 100 defective units that were missed by the inspection process. You will end up unwittingly shipping these 100 defective units to your customer!

The right approach is to prevent defects from occurring in the first place. Then there is no need to spend a lot of time and money trying to find them with ineffective inspection methods.

WORDS OF CAUTION

As an organization becomes more prevention focused, the occurrence of big and urgent problems—usually called "fires"—will diminish. This can result in a new problem—management complacency. As "firefighting" ceases to exist, management may eventually become impervious to the prevention benefits. They may begin to ask, "Why do we need all of these people

---

1. See Joseph M. Juran, A. Blanton Godfrey, eds. 1999. *Juran's Quality Handbook*, Fifth Ed. New York: McGraw-Hill.

when we don't have problems anymore?" In fact, management may begin to think that some of the prevention activities are not necessary anymore and are really a waste of time. The situation can best be described by the analogy of firefighters versus fire prevention professionals. See Figure 2.7.

Firefighters are heroes who are regarded with much respect, admiration, and appreciation. Everything about them is glamorous. They race down the road in a bright red fire truck with the sirens blaring. They wear an impressive uniform with a big hat and coat, boots, and sometimes even special equipment such as an oxygen mask and special vision eyewear. They break down

Firefighting	Prevention
*Urgent	*Important
*Reactive	*Proactive
*Defense	*Offense

Mike Kemp/RubberBall Productions/Getty Images

RubberBall/RubberBall Productions/Getty Images

Figure 2.7   Firefighting vs. prevention.

doors, bring in the powerful water hoses, and rescue the old folks and babies.

When the fire is extinguished and the babies are rescued, everyone cheers and applauds the firefighters. Those firefighters receive praise and glory during the evening news broadcast. And I would bet that their budget is pretty secure for next year and beyond.

Then we have the poor fire prevention folks. They are kind of a quiet breed, but they can really be a pain in the rear end. They put restrictions on how much you can store and where you can store it. They put ugly sprinkler heads in the ceilings. They require fire extinguishers to be hung on the walls. They restrict what materials can be used in buildings. They make you do fire drills, usually at the most inopportune times. Nobody really appreciates them. Yet, which group really saves more lives and waste in the long run?

So, how does one impress upon management the importance and value of continuing prevention activities? The answer is maintaining performance metrics.

ARM YOURSELF WITH PERFORMANCE METRICS

It is absolutely imperative that appropriate performance metrics (measures) be maintained to measure the improvement trends that are a direct result of prevention activities. When it is demonstrated that the relatively small investment in prevention has resulted in a large dollar return in the form of reduced failure costs, shorter lead times, and improved schedule adherence, management will support the prevention investment. It is important that performance trends, such as 12-month averages that are reported each month, be routinely plotted and reported to management as a constant demonstration of the continuous substantial returns that result from the investment in prevention. Only with this continued demonstration will management continue to stay on board.

Improvement is best measured by the reduction in costs required to provide the customer with excellent product. The single best metric for measuring prevention effectiveness is the total cost of quality. Any cost that would not have been expended had quality been perfect contributes to the cost of quality. The costs associated with doing things over because of quality failures are significant, and they offer an opportunity for quality improvement, cost reduction, schedule improvement, and profit improvement.

3

Consumer Focus

It's all about building consumer loyalty.

EARN AND KEEP CONSUMER LOYALTY

Customer vs. Consumer

The customer is the party who directly purchases your product. The consumer is the ultimate user of your product. In some cases the customer may also be the user, but often this is not the case. Obviously the customer is an important stakeholder, and the customer's satisfaction with your product and service is likewise important. However, it is the consumer who is the most important. The primary focus must always be the consumer. Success with consumers drives success with customers.

There are also important internal customers within your company who are actually consumers (users) of products or services from their internal suppliers. A discussion on internal customers and internal suppliers is provided at the end of this chapter in the section entitled "Drive Effective Supplier–Customer Communication."

Consumer Requirements

Quality means conformance to requirements. If a product or service conforms to all of the requirements, then it is a quality product or service. The requirements, however, must be consumer focused. The majority of quality problems are due to poor requirements/specifications. Efforts to improve quality often fail because the consumer's needs and requirements are poorly understood and therefore are not reflected in the company's specifications. Much attention and effort need to be focused on understanding the needs of the consumer.

Communicating Requirements

Even in situations where the requirements are responsive to the consumer's needs, if the requirements are not adequately communicated and fully understood, then efforts to deliver quality and earn consumer loyalty will undoubtedly fail. Only when the company's specifications are consumer-responsive and fully communicated and understood will true quality achievement have a chance. When conforming to consumer requirements becomes an integral part of company culture, consumer loyalty will begin to be built. Consumer loyalty is what drives company success.

UNDERSTAND FORESEEABLE USE

A very important factor in determining consumer requirements is assessing reasonably foreseeable consumer use and misuse of the product. This relates to things like consumer assembly required, product operation, product instructions, packaging and product removal from packaging, product labeling, safety concerns and warnings, different use environments, expected product life, and alternative consumer uses.

Minimize Assembly

The consumer-friendly approach, naturally, is to eliminate or minimize consumer assembly. Any assembly that is required must be simple and obvious, easy (requiring a low level of forces and coordination), and such that misassembly is either impossible or easily corrected. If general tools are required, then this information should be conspicuously stated on the package. If special tools are required, then they should be provided with the product.

Make Product Operation Obvious

Proper operation of the product by the consumer must be intuitive and foolproof. For example, turning knobs in a clockwise direction should increase intensity, and turning counterclockwise should decrease intensity. Any accidental misoperation must not permanently damage the product or render it nonfunctional.

The assembly and operation of the product should be so easy and obvious that instructions are not even required, or are at least greatly simplified.

Minimize Packaging

Packaging should be minimized because it is expensive and ultimately wasteful. Use only enough to protect the product from damage during shipment, handling, and storage and to provide necessary communication about the product to the consumer. The packaging must also be convenient and safe for the consumer to remove. At times packaging may also be required to prevent pilfering of component parts.

Eliminate Warnings

Product warnings are often ineffective, either because they are not read or because the consumer is not motivated or able to change their behavior. The correct approach is to eliminate the hazard and any need for a warning. Any product labeling that is needed, such as apparel care and content, should be simple, clear, and legible.

Substantiate Claims

A claim is any representation, whether stated or implied, concerning any product or service attribute. This includes representations of appearance, size, weight, content, operation, use, and performance.

For example, if a declaration of net weight appears on the package of the product, then it must be verified and documented that the production process is delivering product that conforms to the net weight claim. This will at a minimum mean verifying that the mean minus one standard deviation of the process is equal to or greater than the declared net weight. This equates to approximately 84 percent of the process population meeting or exceeding the declared weight. Sometimes two or even three standard deviations, instead of just one, might be desired and specified, depending on the type of claim and its importance to the consumer.

Please refer to Chapter 4, "Process Capability," for an explanation of process mean and standard deviation and how they relate to defective rate and specification conformance.

It is very important that all product and service representations to the consumer be accurate and substantiated with testing data and information. Consumer delight results from exceeding expectations and delivering more than was promised. Never exaggerate or fail to substantiate any claim directed to the consumer.

Consider All Possible Environments

It should be recognized that the product will be used in various environments. The product may see environments of extreme temperatures, varying levels of humidity, rain, fog, sunshine and ultraviolet radiation, salt water, dust, and even ozone. The requirements must ensure that the product is designed and manufactured to withstand reasonably foreseeable environments of consumer use.

Ensure Adequate Product Life

Product reliability is a critical component of consumer loyalty. It is vital that the product be designed, manufactured, tested, and verified against life requirements that exceed the expectation of the consumer. Since there can be significant consumer variation in expected life, a conservative approach with a factor of safety in the life requirements is necessary. A product safety rule of thumb is to test and qualify components for three times the normal lifetime of the product.

Beware of Alternative Uses

An awareness of alternative uses is especially important when establishing requirements for children's products. The design review process should include an assessment of reasonably foreseeable ways the product might be used that go beyond the intended use. For example, a large inflatable ball might be used (misused) by the consumer as a safety flotation device in a swimming pool. This must be considered in the way the product is designed and labeled.

Another example is childproof caps for adult medicine containers. Even though the container is clearly intended for adults, it is known that some children will try to use the product in imitation of the parent.

BUILD BRANDS, NOT COMMODITIES

Quality is not about industry standards. While satisfying industry standards might be a company requirement, it is clearly not enough. If you rely only on industry standards when establishing your requirements, then you are really treating your product as a commodity. Once you begin treating your product as a commodity, then there is no product differentiation or brand value. The emphasis must always be on consumer requirements and consumer-focused standards.

A strong brand name provides a huge competitive advantage. Consumers are loyal to strong brands, and they are willing to pay more for a name they can trust. To build brand value and consumer loyalty, it is absolutely imperative to have a company culture of 100 percent responsiveness to the consumer. Meeting generic industry standards is just not enough. Focus on developing your own special standards that go beyond industry standards and that will result in delighting the consumer and differentiating your product from all of the generic stuff out there. Building brand value is all about constantly serving and delighting the consumer. It is all about the consumer. The consumer determines your success.

HIGH QUALITY MEANS HIGH PROFITABILITY

High product quality is the key to profitability. The good news is that everyone is theoretically in favor of high quality. Unfortunately, an exception sometimes occurs when a product is in high demand and there is a supply shortage. It is interesting how relatively unimportant quality can become to management when a product is selling well and is in short supply. When this situation changes, however, and the supply exceeds the demand, quality becomes of paramount importance again, and then it never seems to be high enough.

Well, high quality must always be the standard! Quality is high only when it is considered high by the consumer.

According to a 1978 research study by the Strategic Planning Institute,[2] quality "has a strong, positive relationship with ROI" (p. 4). The study also concludes, ". . . businesses selling high-quality products and services are generally more profitable than those with lower-quality offerings" (p. 2). Figure 3.1 summarizes this finding, which was based on the combined experience of more than 1000 businesses. Not only do both ROI and net profit increase as relative quality increases, but the greatest impact on profitability is at the highest quality level.

This study also looked at the effect of combinations of market share and quality on profitability. Figure 3.2 shows that high quality is positively related to ROI independent of market share. It also shows that the combination of high quality and high market share produced an ROI that was more than three

2. Robert D. Buzzell. 1978. *Product Quality*. Cambridge, MA: Strategic Planning Institute.

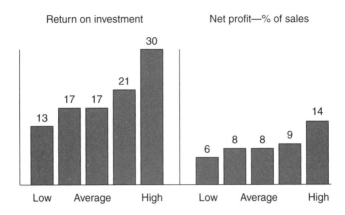

Source: The Strategic Planning Institute study of 1200 businesses in 1978

Figure 3.1   Product quality and profitability.

times greater than the ROI of the low-quality, low-market-share businesses.

High-quality businesses generally charge higher prices than average-quality and low-quality businesses. High-quality businesses also generally have lower total cost structures than other businesses. This is why high quality and high profitability are related. However, high-quality businesses can also achieve greater growth and market share with a combination of high quality and moderate price premium over their major competition. As we see in Figure 3.2, both high quality and

Source: The Strategic Planning Institute study of 1200 Businesses in 1978

Figure 3.2   Product quality, market share, and return on investment.

high market share are a powerful combination for maximum ROI. Whatever the strategy, the one common denominator for profitability is high product quality.

DRIVE EFFECTIVE SUPPLIER–CUSTOMER COMMUNICATION

The key to productivity is to stop doing nonproductive work. Stop investing labor and material resources in producing output that is of little or no value to your customers. This requires that you identify your customers and the output they need from your function. Only when you clearly understand your customers' requirements will you be able to ensure that your function is adding value.

Likewise, it is important to ensure that your suppliers clearly understand your requirements, so their output will be of value to you. Effective supplier–customer communication begins to occur when there is a mutual agreement on valid, specific, and quantitative input requirements.

Each employee is a customer of output from another employee. Each employee also has a customer or customers to whom he or she provides input. As Figure 3.3 shows, the process is simply taking an input from a supplier and adding value to this input to create an output that is useful to your customer. Quality measures must be established with your suppliers and customers to show that supplier output always meets customer requirements.

The primary responsibility of managers is ensuring the quality of output from their areas. Managers must accept responsibility for the output of their areas and establish the standards and measures for quality.

It is important to observe customers in their own environment to understand what processes they perform with your output. The key is in understanding the "what" and the "why" of

Supplier   Employee/Department   Customer

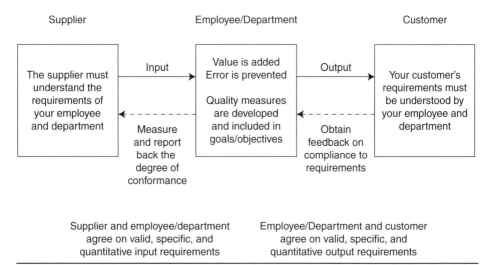

Figure 3.3 Productivity through supplier–customer communication.

their process—what is done and why it is done. Focusing on the customer's end of the process will help you understand the customer's real requirements.

This concept can be summed up nicely by paraphrasing the late Peter Drucker: Quality in a product or service is not what the supplier puts in. It is what the customer gets out and is willing to pay for. Customers pay only for what is of use to them and gives them value. Nothing else is quality.

4

Process Capability

A successful mission depends on capable processes.

REQUIRE CAPABLE PROCESSES BEFORE PRODUCTION STARTS

Imagine that you are on that space shuttle blasting off into outer space. The mission to bring you safely back to Earth, I'm guessing, would be of vital importance to you.

Now imagine the thousands of processes that must be successful to ensure mission success. How would you feel knowing that one or more of the processes might not be capable of meeting the requirements for a successful mission?

Clearly, everyone would want to be totally sure that each and every one of the processes is absolutely capable before getting on that shuttle and starting the mission. Likewise, before beginning the production of any product, it is first necessary to verify that all critical processes are capable of meeting the requirements.

A process should meet three criteria for capability:

1. The process is completely defined and documented

2. The process is *centered*, meaning the calculated average of the process output is equal to the specification requirement

3. The process has *acceptable variation*, meaning the width of the process (the range of the calculated high and low values) is reasonably less than the width of the specification (the difference between the upper specification tolerance limit and the lower specification tolerance limit)

These criteria will be defined and described throughout the next five sections.

DEFINE AND DOCUMENT THE PROCESS

The first step to ensuring process capability is to completely define the process. All relevant processing conditions must be documented, including specific materials used; exact equipment used; precise equipment settings (and equipment calibration verification); all processing sequence steps including processing parameters such as times, temperatures, pressures, and so forth; all operator procedures and methods used; and a processing facility description including ambient conditions.

The process documentation must describe essentially everything about the process inputs and processing activities that produced the output that is tested and evaluated. In fact, without the process first being fully defined and documented, the testing and evaluation of the output should not occur. Process capability has not occurred if the process has not been completely defined and documented.

The process documentation from a well-defined, capable process becomes a valuable benchmark tool for future use. If the process output ever changes for no apparent reason, the process capability documentation will likely provide key information and insight for quick diagnosis and corrective action. Without this information, corrective action could be very time-consuming and costly.

TEST TO FAILURE, NOT TO SPECIFICATION

An important requirement for determining process capability is to test to failure, as opposed to just testing to the specification value. If you just test to the specification, then you will not know if the process is centered and has acceptable variation. You must test to failure to determine when these two criteria are satisfied. Production must not begin until process capability is verified.

It is surprising just how often companies test to specification when evaluating whether conformance to the specification has been achieved. For example, if the specification for the pull strength (tensile strength) of a button attached (sewn) to a young child's garment is 20 pounds, it is not unusual to observe the test being performed to the 20-pound value and then being stopped to record the successful 20-pound pull test. It is also not unusual to see this test performed on relatively few samples, often 10 or 20, or sometimes even just 1. This is a big problem.

If 20 samples are tested to the specification and zero nonconformances are observed, have we demonstrated zero defects? What can we accurately state about the strength and integrity of the button attachment process? All we can say is that we are 90 percent confident that the expected failure rate is less than approximately 10 percent. This can be readily determined by using the table in Figure 4.1. Using the row corresponding to a sample size of 20 and finding the column for the upper 90 percent confidence limit, we see that the population percent defective could be as high as 10 percent (at 95 percent confidence, it could be up to 13 percent).

Now, assume that the specification for the button pull test is required to ensure that a small child will not be exposed to an accessible small button that can create a choking hazard. Is "less than 10 percent expected failure rate" an acceptable

Population % defective—upper limit estimate		
Sample size	90% confidence	95% confidence
5	35%	40%
10	20%	24%
15	14%	17%
20	10%	13%
30	7%	9%
50	4.4%	5.7%
100	2.3%	2.9%
250	0.9%	1.2%
1000	0.23%	0.30%

Figure 4.1 Population percent defective when sample percent defective is zero.

result? Has it really been demonstrated that a small child will be protected from a choking injury by the attachment process?

The answer is no. Figure 4.1 shows that even if 1000 samples were tested to the specification, the expected failure rate might still be too far above zero (0.23%). So what should we do?

The answer is to test to failure. Only when you test to failure will you know how good or bad your process really is. Since we know that the results of measurement and test data typically fall into a normal or bell-shaped distribution, we can calculate expected failure rates using the normal distribution, or normal curve.

PITCHING THE NORMAL CURVE

The normal distribution, also known as the normal curve or the bell curve because of its shape, is a very special distribution for the following reasons:

1. *It is prevalent*—It is known that measurements (length, width, height, weight, density, area, volume, and so forth) from a given population or process are generally normally distributed. This means if you measure every unit from the population or process and plot these measurements on a chart with the horizontal axis (X-axis) as the measurement and the vertical axis (Y-axis) as the frequency or number of units with that corresponding X-axis measurement, then the plot of measurement values will form a normal, or bell, curve. The following are just a few of the many examples of normally distributed populations:

   –The heights of adult males in the United States

   –The intelligence quotients (IQs) of adult Americans

   –The weight (density) of fabric coming off a weaving loom that is "in control"—running without any special causes of variation

–The lengths of sleeves coming off an automated cutting process, before being sewn into garments

–The net weights of cans of Play-Doh brand modeling compound coming off a production line that is in control

2. *It is relatively simple*—The normal curve is a two-parameter distribution; the two parameters are the mean and the standard deviation. The mean is simply the average, and it is usually designated by the term $\overline{X}$. The standard deviation is simply a measure of dispersion, or how far most of the values are from the mean. It is usually designated by the term σ (sigma). Every normal distribution can be totally described by these two parameters, the mean and the standard deviation. If two normal curves have the same mean and standard deviation, then they are identical normal distributions.

3. *It is very useful*—The mean and standard deviation of a sample randomly taken from a normally distributed population are unbiased estimates of the population mean and standard deviation. Therefore, what is learned from the sample becomes applicable to the population. We can draw powerful conclusions about a population or process based on what we learn from a sample. This will be further described and demonstrated in the next sections of this chapter.

Figure 4.2 shows a normal curve with a mean equal to zero and a standard deviation equal to one. This is called a *standard normal distribution*. You can see that approximately 68 percent of the values fall between +1 standard deviation and –1 standard deviation. This is true for every normal curve, no matter what the mean or standard deviation. You will always find the same 68 percent in the range formed by the mean $+1\sigma$ and the mean -1σ.

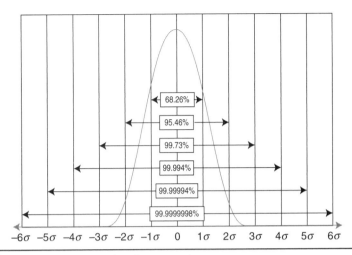

Figure 4.2   Areas under the normal curve.

As you can see in Figure 4.2, approximately 95 percent of the population values will always fall between +2 and –2 standard deviations added to the mean, and +3 and –3 standard deviations will always contain about 99.7 percent of the population values. Figure 4.2 arbitrarily stops at +6 and –6 standard deviations. This is sometimes referred to as Six Sigma. Only 0.0000002% (two parts per billion) of the values fall outside the Six Sigma limits. Therefore, Six Sigma quality means two parts per billion defective.

MEASURE AND VERIFY PROCESS CAPABILITY

Process capability is sometimes designated by the term *Cp* (capability of process), and it is defined as specification width divided by process width. Specification width is just the difference between the upper specification tolerance limit and the lower specification tolerance limit. Process width is the difference between the process mean plus three standard deviations (3σ) and the process mean minus three standard deviations, or a total of six standard deviations of process variation. Figure 4.3 illustrates the concept of Cp.

Cp is a good measure of process capability only when the process is centered. A process is centered when the process mean is equal to the specification target. Although centering the process should always be an objective, it doesn't always happen. Therefore, a process capability factor with a correction for noncentering is used: Cpk. Cpk is the difference between the process mean and the nearest specification tolerance limit divided by one-half the process width. Cpk is a good measure of process capability because it accounts for noncentering and

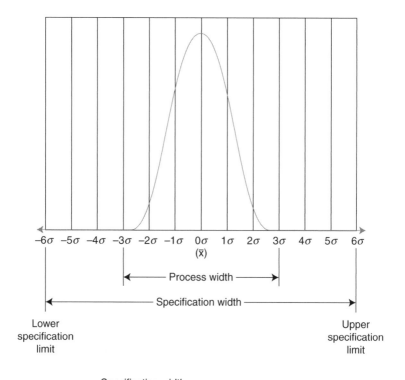

$$Cp = \frac{\text{Specification width}}{\text{Process width}}$$

$$= \frac{6\sigma - (-6\sigma)}{3\sigma - (-3\sigma)} = \frac{12\sigma}{6\sigma} = \frac{12}{6} = 2$$

Figure 4.3   The concept of Cp.

therefore can be related directly to process output defective rate. Cpk and Cp are equal only when the process is centered. The only real value of using Cp is to determine the maximum potential Cpk to be realized by correcting a noncentered process. Figure 4.4 illustrates the concept of Cpk.

SIGNIFICANCE OF CPK

When the Cpk of a process is known, we know what to expect for process output defective rate. Figures 4.5 shows some relationships of Cpk to defective rate. For a given specification tolerance, there are only two ways to increase process capability (in other words, decrease process defective rate). One is to center the process. The other is to reduce the inherent variation (σ) of the process. Centering the process is much quicker and

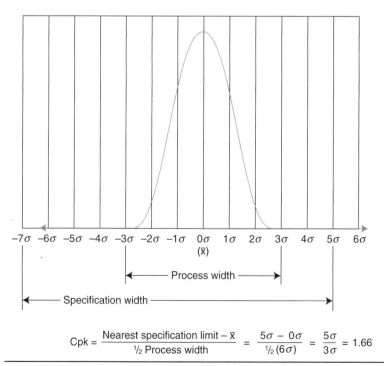

$$Cpk = \frac{\text{Nearest specification limit} - \bar{x}}{\text{½ Process width}} = \frac{5\sigma - 0\sigma}{\text{½}(6\sigma)} = \frac{5\sigma}{3\sigma} = 1.66$$

Figure 4.4 The concept of Cpk.

Cpk	Defective rate
0.33	32%
0.66	5%
1.00	0.27%
1.33	60 ppm
1.66	0.6 ppm
2.00	2 ppb

Figure 4.5   Relationship of Cpk to defective rate.

easier to do than reducing process variation and should be done first. Reducing process variation requires applying design of experiments (DOE) tools to determine the main factors contributing to the variation and then making process changes in response to the DOE findings. This should only be done after you have made sure the process is centered.

Looking at Figure 4.6 at the row where Cp is equal to 1.33, we can see that the effect of the process being off center by two standard deviations is a Cpk of 0.66. Figure 4.5 shows that a Cpk of 0.66 equates to a defective rate of 5%. By just centering the process, the Cpk would improve to 1.33 and the defective rate would improve over eightyfold to 60 parts per million!

Comparing the Cpk to the Cp highlights opportunities for improvement by centering the process. The greater the difference between the two, the greater the opportunity for centering.

Cp	Centered Cpk	Off by 1σ Cpk	off by 2σ Cpk
1.00	1.00	0.66	0.33
1.33	1.33	1.00	0.66
1.66	1.66	1.33	1.00
2.00	2.00	1.66	1.33

Figure 4.6   Relationship of Cpk to Cp when process is centered and when shifted off specification by 1σ and 2σ.

Summing it up, the first step in determining process capability is either taking measurements or testing to failure, depending on the type of process characteristic being evaluated. Then we can calculate the mean and make sure the process is centered on the specification. Next we calculate the standard deviation and determine how many standard deviations are contained within the specification tolerances. This allows us to calculate the Cpk, relate it to failure rate, and determine whether the process is capable of meeting our quality requirements. That's all there is to process capability verification. Once we determine that the process is capable, we then need to control the process to ensure no changes or special causes of variation occur. Process control is covered in the next chapter.

CONTROL ACCURACY AND PRECISION

To fully understand process capability, it is important to understand the difference between accuracy and precision. *Accuracy* is the characteristic of a measurement that indicates how close an observed value is to the true value. To simplify, think of it as the difference between the observed and the true. You can think of it as a positional measure, much like the mean is a positional measure of a process.

Precision is the characteristic of a measurement that relates to consistency and repeatability. To simplify, think of precision as measurement variation. Whereas accuracy relates to a process mean, precision relates to a process standard deviation. Figure 4.7 describes pictorially the concepts of accuracy and precision.

Calibration for Accuracy

Verifying process capability applies to more than just the production process. For example, it also applies to the test and measurement processes. Obviously, the equipment must be

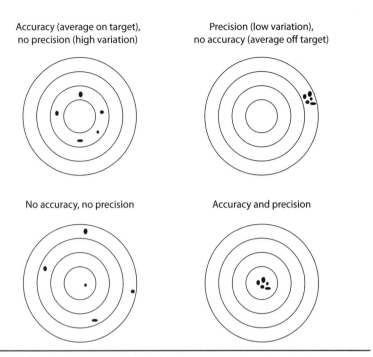

Figure 4.7   Accuracy and precision.

calibrated. But is calibration enough? Calibration means comparing a measurement system of unknown accuracy to a measurement system of known accuracy in order to detect any deviation from the required standard. This means you can think of calibration as a check for accuracy. But what about precision? Both accuracy and precision are important. How are test and measurement system precision measured?

Gage R&R for Precision

Gage repeatability and reproducibility (Gage R&R) evaluates the measurement variation (error) in a measurement system. There are two components: gage variation (repeatability) and operator variation (reproducibility). If the percentage of the specification tolerance consumed by the Gage R&R (measurement variation) does not exceed 10 percent, then the measurement system is excellent. If it exceeds 10 percent but is less than 30 percent, then it may be adequate for situations where the Cpk is high. The point is, Gage R&R is to measurement precision what calibration is to measurement accuracy. Both are important and should be verified.

Both accuracy and precision are necessary for describing measurement events, just as both the mean and the standard deviation are necessary for describing a normal distribution.

THE PRECISION OF NUMBERS

There is a story about a security guard at a museum who overhears two folks wondering just how old the dinosaur bones are that they are viewing. The security guard responds that the bones are exactly four million and four years, two months, and six days old. When the folks ask in amazement how the security guard can be so exact in his answer, he responds, "Well, they were four million years old when I started working here, and I've been here exactly four years, two months, and six days." Obviously, the dinosaur bones are only *approximately* four million years old, maybe somewhere between 3.9 and 4.1 million years old. The length of time that the security guard has been employed at the museum (four years, two months, and six days) is insignificant compared to the estimated age of the dinosaur bones. Therefore, adding the guard's employment time to the estimated age of the bones results in an erroneous answer (and a humorous story).

This is a good example of implying much more precision in a mathematical result than is reasonable, given the precision of the individual measurements used in the calculation. The results of mathematical operations performed with given numbers can be no more precise than the original numbers themselves. It is therefore necessary to recognize and express the proper number of significant figures when working with data so the result doesn't imply greater precision than was originally obtained in the numbers used to calculate that result.

Figure 4.8 provides the rules for determining the significant figures in a number.

Rule	Example	Number of significant figures
1. All non-zero digits are significant	12.1	3
2. All zeros between two non-zero digits are significant	102.01	5
3. All zeros to the left of an understood (not written) decimal point but to the right of a non-zero digit are not significant	1200	2
4. All zeros to the left of an expressed (written) decimal point and to the right of a non-zero digit are significant	1200.	4
5. All zeros to the right of a decimal point but to the left of a non-zero digit are not significant	0.0012	2
6. All zeros to the right of a decimal point and also to the right of a non-zero digit are significant	0.012000	5

Addition and Subtraction Operations

First, round off all measurements or values to the number of decimal places in the measurement with the fewest decimal places, then add or subtract.

Example: Add 1.2 ft., 12.12 ft., and 0.121 ft.

Solution: (Round off and add)   1.2 ft.
                                              12.1 ft.
                                               0.1 ft.
Answer: 13.4 ft.

Multiplication and Division Operations

In general, first multiply (or divide) the values. Then round off the product (or remainder) to the same number of significant figures as the value having the fewer significant figures.

Example: Multiply 1.2 ft. X 12.12 ft. X 0.121 ft.

Solution: 1.2 ft. X 12.12 ft. X 0.121 ft. = 1.759824 ft.

Answer: 1.8 ft. (Round off to two significant figures)

Mean and Standard Deviation

Record the mean to one more significant figure than the raw data. Record the standard deviation to the same number of decimal places as the mean.

Figure 4.8   Rules for significant figures.

APPLY FACTORS OF SAFETY

A traditional definition of *factor of safety* is minimum strength divided by maximum stress. For example, refer to Figure 4.9, and imagine it is you who is dangling from that cliff and relying on a safety line. If we assume that you weigh 175 pounds and that you might exert a dynamic load of twice your weight

$$\text{Safety Factor} = \frac{\text{Minimum Strength (of your safety line)}}{\text{Maximum Stress (exerted by your weight)}}$$

Figure 4.9 Factor of safety for safety line.

during a slip, then the safety line should be rated at a minimum of 350 pounds. If the line is rated at exactly 350 pounds, then you have a factor of safety of 1, since minimum strength and maximum stress are equal. However, would you be comfortable in this situation with a safety factor of only 1? You would probably want a safety factor of at least 10—maybe even 20 or more if you have a fear of heights!

Factors of safety allow for uncertainty in the design and manufacturing process, and they are essentially compensations for imperfection. They are commonly used in the design and engineering stages of product creation. The point is, you must have a factor of safety significantly greater than 1 applied to your internal standards to ensure that you are working to requirements that exceed any mandatory regulations. This is especially important in product safety compliance areas. There is too much uncertainty in variations affecting design, material, fabrication, packaging, testing equipment, testing procedure, transportation, and handling to make your internal standards equal to the outside mandatory requirements. It is up to you to choose the safety factor that is appropriate for your product and business, but it should always be greater than 1. In situations or conditions that involve varying degrees of uncertainty, you may want to consider safety factors of 3, 5, or even 10 or higher.

5

Process Control

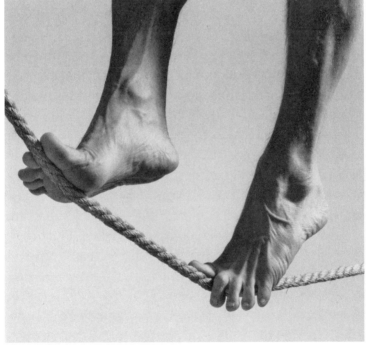

Tim Flach/Stone/Getty Images

Maintain balance and control with
precise, timely adjustments.

AVOID TYPE 1 AND TYPE 2 ERRORS

The tightrope walker can be used to represent the concept of process control. Imagine that one end of the tightrope is connected to the top of a 9-story building. The other end is connected to the top of a 10-story building that is 50 feet away. The objective is to walk on the tightrope from one building to the other (without falling off).

Think of the rope as the specification; of course, we want to stay on the specification. A defect is falling off of the rope. The process is the activity of walking on the rope from one building to the other. We really want the process to deliver zero defects! How will that happen?

As we begin the journey along the tightrope, we obviously need to make body-position adjustments to maintain our balance. The extent and timing of these adjustments is critical to achieving zero defects. For example, if a gust of wind comes up, we must counteract it with body adjustments to maintain balance. With experience, this might become instinctual.

What happens, however, if you do not make any adjustments when the gust of wind occurs? You fall off. This is an example of a Type 2 error. A Type 2 error occurs when a "special cause" change occurs but no action is taken. In this case, the gust of wind is the special cause. Since there was no action taken (no adjustment) and a change occurred (the gust of wind), the process created a defect (falling off).

What happens if you mistakenly imagine there is a gust of wind? You fall off. This is an example of a Type 1 error. A Type 1 error occurs when there is not a special cause of variation (change), but action is taken because a change is imagined. Since action was taken (a shift of weight) but no change occurred (no gust of wind), the process created a defect (again, falling off).

The next section relates Type 1 and Type 2 errors to process tampering and process neglect.

AVOID TAMPERING AND NEGLECT

To achieve zero defects, you must control the process after it has been verified as being capable. Controlling a process requires periodically testing a small product sample and recording the results on a control chart. There are two important reasons for doing this:

1. To prevent *tampering* with the process

2. To prevent *neglecting* the process

Tampering with a process means making an adjustment to a process that is operating without any special causes of variation. The only variations present are *common causes*, meaning they are inherent in the process. Process tampering is obviously associated with Type 1 errors. Tampering with a process results in increased variation and defects. Process control charts can identify when there has been no special cause change and when the process must be left alone. They can prevent the Type 1 errors associated with process tampering.

Neglecting a process means not making an adjustment to a process when something has caused it to change. This relates to a Type 2 error. Neglecting a process results in increased variation and defects. The use of process control charts identifies when a change (special cause of variation) has occurred so the change can be corrected without producing defective product. Without process control charts, the change probably would not be readily apparent and defective product could unwittingly be produced and shipped to the consumer. Process control charts can prevent the Type 2 errors associated with process neglect.

IDENTIFY CRITICAL PROCESS CHARACTERISTICS

It is important to realize that certainly not all process characteristics need to be controlled during production. Only a vital few

process characteristics need to be considered. This can sometimes mean isolating just one critical process characteristic.

From the Pareto principle, we know that 20 percent or
fewer of the causes produce 80 percent or more of the effect.
Generally, when there is a process output problem to be solved,
the number-one cause can account for more than 50 percent
of the solution. The number-one and number-two causes combined often account for more than 75 percent of the solution.
The top three causes combined can account for 90 percent or
more. These major causes are generally discovered using DOE
methods.

Please refer to the section titled "From Causes to Vital Root
Causes" in Chapter 7.

Once the vital causes are identified, they can best be controlled during production using the process control method
described in the next section—precontrol.

ENFORCE PRECONTROL AND POSITROL

Once a process has been determined to be capable of meeting
the requirements, it is important to control the process, thereby
preventing the manufacture of defects. Controlling a process is
just charting the process output and taking the action indicated
by the charted results. The action indicated by the chart will be
to leave the process alone, adjust the process while it is running, or stop the process for adjustment and for another process
capability verification (also called a requalification).

The control chart is the tool that aids in preventing Type 1
errors (tampering with the process) and Type 2 errors (neglecting the process). The control chart guides us in knowing when
a change is occurring that requires a process adjustment to prevent the process from making defective product.

The control chart serves to alert us to the two kinds of
changes that can occur to the process output: (1) a change in

process centering (the process average) and (2) a change to process variation (the process standard deviation). As previously discussed, process measurement data generally are normally distributed.

The normal distribution is a two-parameter distribution: one parameter is the mean and the other is the standard deviation. If the mean and standard deviation of the process are known, then everything important about the process is known. The process changes when the mean or the standard deviation (or both) changes.

Precontrol is the best process control method in terms of simplicity and power. It can be taught to an operator in 10 minutes, and it can help keep processes running hundreds of thousands and even millions of units without a single defect. The only requirement is that the process be capable at a Cpk of 1.33 or higher. This Cpk requirement must be verified prior to the approval of the process. Note that although a minimum Cpk of 1.33 is required for precontrol, one should really strive for Cpk's of 2, 3, 4, and higher.

Precontrol is described in four steps as follows.

Step 1: Set Up Precontrol Chart Zones

The specification width is divided by 4 to create the precontrol zones as shown in Figure 5.1. The zone created by the middle half of the specification width is designated as the green zone. The two zones on either side of the green zone are designated as the yellow zones. The two zones beyond the yellow zones are designated as the red zones.

Step 2: Qualify the Process

At process start-up, take five consecutive units from the process. If all five fall within the green zone, then the process is qualified and production can begin. Proceed to step 3. However, if one or more of the units falls outside of the green zone, then

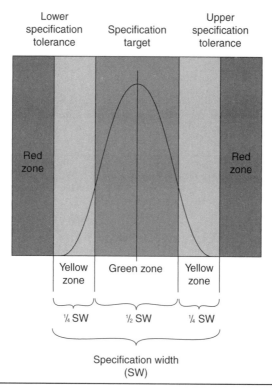

Figure 5.1 Precontrol zones.

the process is not qualified. The cause of the variation must be determined and reduced or eliminated. After this is done, begin step 2 again to verify process qualification.

Step 3: Begin Precontrol Charting

After production begins, take two consecutive units from the process every half-hour, record the results, and proceed according to the following rules:

1. If both units are in the green zone, continue production.

2. If one unit is in the green zone and the other is in the yellow zone, continue production.

3. If both units are in the same yellow zone, adjust the process while continuing to run production.

4. If each unit falls into a different yellow zone, stop production. The cause of variation must be determined and reduced or eliminated. After this is done, begin step 2 again.

5. If one or both units are in the red zone, stop production. The cause of variation must be determined and reduced or eliminated. After this is done, begin step 2 again.

Step 4: Adjust the Frequency of Precontrol Sampling

The frequency of sampling is adjusted based on dividing the average time period between two production stoppages by six. For example, if production was stopped because the two units were in opposite yellow zones and then stopped again six hours later because a unit was in the red zone, then the time period of six hours between stoppages is divided by six to give a sampling frequency of every one hour. If the period between stoppages was six days, then the sampling frequency would be once a day.

Although you can certainly choose to increase the sampling frequency by applying a number larger than six in the denominator, it is not necessary in most applications. However, it is recommended that sampling occur at start-up after any process stoppage.

While that is all there is to precontrol, there is another process control tool that should be used in concert with precontrol. That tool is Positrol.

Positive Control with Positrol

Positrol is used together with precontrol to ensure that important processing conditions are maintained at optimum during production. The Positrol chart identifies *what* processing parameters will be measured along with the specifications and tolerances, *who* will do the measuring, *how* and *where* the measurements will be taken, and *when* they will be taken.

For example, perhaps processing temperature and time are important in a drying process. The temperature (what) of the oven chamber entrance (where) is to be measured using a thermocouple potentiometer (how) by the laboratory technician (who) at the start of the shift (when). The specification is 350°F +/– 10°F. The drying time/conveyor belt speed (what) is to be measured using a stopwatch to measure drying cycle (how) by the laboratory technician (who) at the start of each shift (when).

The Positrol chart, therefore, is just a who, what, how, where, and when log that is monitored by the process engineer or supervisor to ensure optimum processing conditions are being maintained.

USE THREE-DIMENSIONAL STANDARDS

When it comes to aesthetics, the best standard is usually a physical product. A production-representative sample is reviewed, approved, and signed off on by both the supplier and the customer. This signed-off sample represents that the manufacturing process is capable of producing product that is aesthetically acceptable to the customer. The signed-off sample also becomes the mutually agreed-upon aesthetic standard for use by the supplier and customer during process and product audits. Signed-off aesthetic samples need to be reviewed and updated, usually once a year, to ensure that no objectionable degradation has occurred.

It can be amusing to watch a visiting customer representative walk through a plant looking at product when no three-dimensional standards are used. Often the person will pick up one or two production units, take a look at them, and then put them back, usually without saying anything. One wonders what they are thinking or considering when they do this. How can a consistent, thorough, and valid assessment be made without a standard, either by the sourcing representative or the producer?

Another benefit of three-dimensional standards is they provide a safety gate for production start and shipping. The approval of the standard serves as the authorization for production start and shipping. Its approval can also be used to represent confirmation of other non-aesthetic characteristics such as materials performance, product performance testing, and so forth. If the aesthetic sample has not been approved, then the supplier must not begin production.

6

Variation Reduction

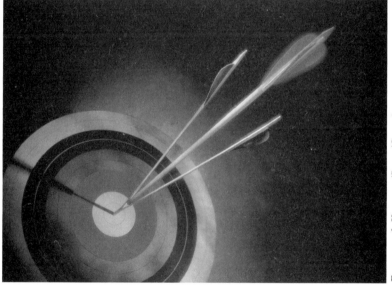

Ferguson & Katzman/Stone/Getty Images

Zero variation means no tolerances are needed.

RECOGNIZE THE EVIL OF VARIATION

Consistency is good. Consistency is splitting the first arrow with the second arrow. Quality is derived through consistency.

Variation is the opposite of consistency. Quality problems result from variation. Specification tolerances are missed because of variation. Parts don't fit because they vary. Schedules are missed because they vary. Consumer satisfaction and delight are not repeated due to variation. Variation is bad.

The target is zero variation, where all of the product is right on specification. Zero variation means no tolerances are needed. Although absolute zero variation is only a theoretical concept, constantly reducing variation must always be a continuous improvement goal. Statistical methods allow us to understand, reduce, and control variation and to eventually conquer it.

CHANGE IS GOOD; VARIATION IS BAD

It is very important not to confuse change with variation. Variation is bad because it represents deviations from a target, specification, or desired result. The goal is always zero variation.

However, change is good when it is planned and directed toward improving a product, process, or service. This kind of change is important and must be a constant in any organization. Change is vital for organizational health and viability. Without change, there would be no improvement, no innovation, no growth, no new world records, and no excitement. Change represents progress and variation represents chaos. Therefore, change and variation in a sense are opposites. Change is good and variation is bad.

DON'T PLAY THE DOGHOUSE
VS. PENTHOUSE GAME

There is a simple statistical fact that must be recognized and observed. It is an important fact if you want to prevent tampering with an organizational process and increasing the amount of variation. (It is also important if you want to prevent looking silly.)

That fact is as follows: There will *always* be an upper 10 percent and a bottom 10 percent in any process, and there is nothing you can do about it. It is normal, natural, and perfectly OK. A corollary is that there will always be an upper 50 percent and a bottom 50 percent, and there is nothing you can do about it.

For example, in any classroom, regardless of how smart the students are, 50 percent of them perform above the classroom median performance level and 50 percent fall below the median performance level. This is a fact, even though most parents seem to think their children are above the median or average for the classroom. The following facetious news headline is presented to emphasize this point:

Parents Outraged That 50% of Students Fall Below Average

We can use U.S. presidents as another example. We can state with complete confidence and accuracy that 50 percent of past U.S. presidents were better than the median and 50 percent were worse than the median. Likewise, there is a top 10 percent and a bottom 10 percent based on any given performance criteria, no matter how great and honorable all of them might have been.

This may seem like an obvious fact, but surprisingly, it is sometimes ignored, forgotten, not practiced, or simply not understood. The best example is the Penthouse list and the Doghouse list, a motivational tactic used by the sales department at a certain company. The top 10 salespeople, based on dollar amount of orders written, made the Penthouse list and received accolades in the company newsletter. The bottom 10 salespeople made the Doghouse list and were somewhat ridiculed and embarrassed in the newsletter.

It didn't matter if the bottom 10 salespeople met or even exceeded their objectives. They were still in the "doghouse."

What sales management didn't fully appreciate was that there would *always* be a "bottom 10," no matter what incentives or punishment they instilled. Their Doghouse and Penthouse game was counterproductive to building department camaraderie and teamwork. What started out as a humorous yet sincere device for motivating the sales team ended up being a total debacle and a demotivator for the team. This unintended consequence was the direct result of sales management not fully appreciating this simple statistical fact.

MOVE FROM ZERO DEFECTS TO ZERO VARIATION

It is interesting how "zero defects" is a very difficult concept for many individuals in many industries to fully understand and accept. People seem to equate zero defects with operator and product perfection. Their response is often something like this:

> How can you expect me to accept the concept of zero defects? I'm working with people here, and no one is perfect. It is unreasonable to expect me to achieve zero defects. That is an unattainable standard.

The answer is to explain what zero defects really means. Zero defects just means that the process output is in the region between the upper specification tolerance limit and the lower specification tolerance limit. This is shown in Figure 6.1.

Once the concept of zero defects is explained in this way, it becomes a little more acceptable to most people. But many will still not be sold on the concept. Then the discussion needs to shift to the concept of zero variation.

Zero variation is a much higher standard than zero defects. In fact, it is really a goal rather than a standard. The goal of zero variation means that even though the process width is fully con-

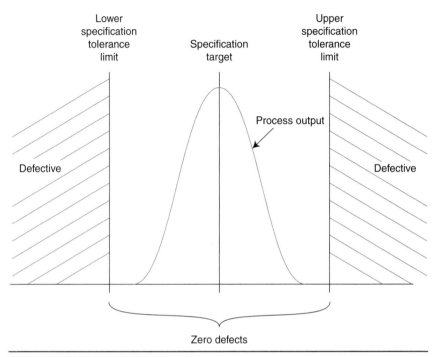

Lower
specification
tolerance
limit

Specification
target

Upper
specification
tolerance
limit

Process output

Defective

Defective

Zero defects

Figure 6.1 The zero defects region.

tained within the specification width, we will continue to reduce the variation. This effort to reduce variation will continue until all process output is essentially right on the specification target. The concept of zero variation is depicted in Figure 6.2.

Once people understand and appreciate the concept of zero variation, they are usually ready to fully accept and embrace the relatively easy standard of zero defects. Of course, the objective is to move from a standard of zero defects to the goal of zero variation. The importance of doing this is explained in the next section.

REMEMBER DR. TAGUCHI

There are two significant problems with the concept of zero defects:

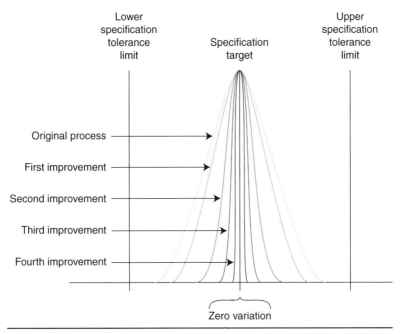

Figure 6.2   Zero variation, the real goal.

1. A measurement that is just barely inside the specification tolerance is considered completely good, but one that is just barely outside the specification tolerance is considered completely bad. In reality, from the consumer's standpoint, there is not a significant difference between the two measurements.

2. The measurement that is just barely inside the specification tolerance is considered to be just as good as a measurement that is right on the specification target. Yet, these two measurements are significantly different.

Dr. Genichi Taguchi, a widely acknowledged leader in the U.S. industrial quality movement, recognized these two problems and addressed them with his quality loss function concept. His loss function recognizes that there is minimum loss with measurements at or near the specification target, and an ever-

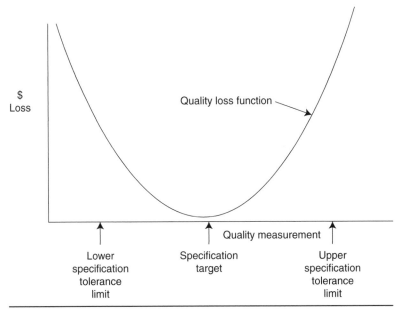

Figure 6.3 The Taguchi loss function.

increasing loss as the measurements depart in either direction from the target. This is shown in Figure 6.3.

Dr. Taguchi shows that the loss (L) increases by the square of the deviation from the specification target value (D^2). He further defines C as representing a constant that is determined by the cost of the countermeasure that the factory might use to get on target. His loss equation is written as $L = D^2C$.

To minimize costs and maximize consumer loyalty, it is important to continually reduce variation and keep the process centered on the specification target. Zero variation is the goal.

7

The Pareto Principle

Paul Katz/Photodisc Green/Getty Images

Focus on the vital few, not on the trivial many.

NOT ALL PROBLEMS ARE CREATED EQUAL

Problems, like opportunities, are unequal in their importance. There are always the most important few, called the vital few, that account for the vast majority of cost or loss. The vital few problems are like the diamonds in the dirt, and our attention and efforts must be focused on them.

It is commonly believed that 20 percent or less of the causes (the vital few) result in 80 percent or more of the effect. This is known as the Pareto principle. This also means that only 20 percent or less of the effect is a result of 80 percent or more of the causes (known as the trivial many). Just as the diamonds represent the vital few, the trivial many are represented by the dirt. Priorities must always be established by isolating the vital few causes or problems from the trivial many.

For example, consider the problem of defective consumer returns. From the Pareto principle we know that approximately 20 percent or less of the product line contributes 80 percent or more of the returns. Further, we know that 20 percent or less of the root causes address 80 percent or more of the total effect (return dollar loss). Therefore, our limited efforts should first be directed to only the top 20 percent of the causes for only the top 20 percent of the types of products returned.

All resources are scarce and precious. There are just not enough resources or enough time to do everything; however, there is always enough time to focus on the vital few problems, root causes, and opportunities. Again, always focus on the diamonds—never waste time playing in the dirt!

FROM SYMPTOMS TO CAUSES

Every problem has associated with it at least one cause and also, usually, many symptoms. If the causes are identified and eliminated, the problem will be eliminated. If only the symptoms are treated, the problem will continue to exist, since symptoms are merely indications of the existence of a problem. It is, therefore, very important to distinguish between causes and symptoms.

FROM CAUSES TO VITAL ROOT CAUSES

Since 20 percent or less of the causes produce 80 percent or more of the effect, it follows that 80 percent or more of the causes produce 20 percent or less of the effect. Figure 7.1 is a typical Pareto chart of causes and their corresponding effects. Note that in this example the number-one cause contributes 50 percent of the total effect. The number-two cause contributes 30 percent of the total effect. And the number-three cause contributes 15 percent of the effect. Also note that the remaining 17-plus causes contribute only 5 percent of the total effect. In this case the top 3 causes represent the vital few root causes, and the other 17-plus causes represent the trivial many.

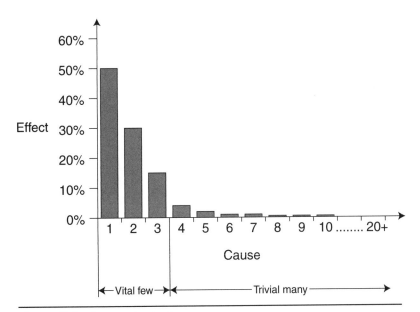

Figure 7.1 Pareto chart of causes.

Discovering the Vital Few Root Causes

There are DOE tools for isolating the vital few root causes from the trivial many causes. When there are more than 20 variables, multi-vari charts can be used to reduce the suspect variables down to a more manageable number. The variables search method is used when there are 5 to 20 variables. A full factorial method is used for 4 or fewer variables. And finally, a B versus C test is used to validate that the vital few causes have been found.

These DOE tools allow you to eliminate the unimportant causes and identify the vital few root causes and how they should be controlled to prevent the problem from ever occurring again. Keki Bhote's outstanding book, *World Class Quality,*[3] provides an excellent presentation of the best DOE tools for filtering out the unimportant variables and homing in on the vital root causes.

PLACE IMPORTANCE OVER URGENCY

When setting priorities, it is important to emphasize the distinction between urgent and important tasks. Urgent tasks compel immediate action, but they may not be important. A ringing telephone is an example. Important tasks strongly affect the course of events, but they may not be urgent. Performing maintenance on your car is an example.

Referring to Figure 7.2, it is obvious that tasks that are both important and urgent will receive the highest priority. Likewise, it is obvious that tasks that are both unimportant and non-urgent

---

3. Keki Bhote and Adi Bhote. 2000. *World Class Quality: Using Design of Experiments to Make It Happen,* 2nd ed. New York: American Management Association.

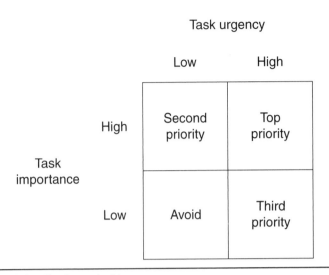

Figure 7.2   Setting priorities.

will receive the lowest priority. In fact, these tasks should be avoided altogether. Just don't do them.

The key point is that tasks that are important and non-urgent should be the second-highest priority, and these tasks must not be sacrificed for the purpose of doing urgent and unimportant tasks. The second-priority quadrant is typically where prevention-oriented projects reside, and these important activities should never take a back seat to tasks in the third-priority quadrant.

CONVERT DATA INTO WISDOM

Nobody likes to read a report containing just data. Data reports do not readily provide any meaning or inspire any action. They are ugly, boring, and a waste of people's time. They often get relegated to the trash can or shredder, which is usually where they belong. So, what should be done with the data being generated that management needs to review and understand?

Those data must be converted into information. This is done by applying the Pareto principle to the data. The objective, once again, is to isolate the vital from the trivial (the diamonds from the dirt). By taking the data, isolating the vital few contributors, and including this in the report, you convert the data into information. The report becomes user-friendly and is much more likely to get management's attention and inspire action. But don't stop there.

The information must be converted into knowledge. This is done by determining the vital few root causes for the variations or variances. By determining and reporting on the root causes, you convert the information into knowledge. You achieve a higher level of understanding, and the report becomes more professional and actionable. However, you are not done yet.

The knowledge must be converted into wisdom. This is done by implementing prevention systems to address the root causes of the variation or variances. When prevention systems are implemented to eliminate errors and variances, you will have achieved the highest level of understanding, called wisdom.

The idea is to always seek a higher level of understanding. You must strive to convert data into information, information into knowledge, and knowledge into wisdom. Figure 7.3 summarizes this concept of the hierarchy of understanding.

LESS IS MORE

Another concept that can be derived from the Pareto principle is that oftentimes less is more. Whether we are referring to reports, memos, specifications, number of component parts, processes, or systems, this is a good principle to keep in mind. Eliminating anything that is unnecessary and irrelevant—including things like words, sentences, data, information, component parts, process steps, movement, transportation, and packaging—results

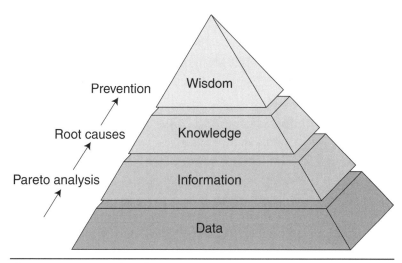

Figure 7.3 Hierarchy of understanding.

in a leaner, simplified, and therefore improved situation. Communication, speed, efficiency, reliability, and cost structure all improve.

The Pareto principle directs us to focus our limited resources on the vital few causes and contributors instead of the trivial many. The "less is more" concept directs us to focus on the vital few items or activities that add the highest value. If it doesn't add significant value, then eliminate it.

PERFORM STRATEGIC AUDITING

Focusing on what is vital also applies to auditing. If one is properly operating in the prevention mode, then the only reason for auditing is to verify that the prevention systems and processes are continuing to function correctly. Auditing should not be performed to control material quality, product quality, or anything else.

Audits should be planned and performed to obtain an adequate amount of information with the minimum amount of effort and cost. Audits are only performed to ensure a reasonable level of confidence that the prevention systems are working. This type of auditing is called strategic auditing, and it is the only type of auditing that should be planned, budgeted, and performed. Any other type of auditing should be immediately stopped.

It is important to note that confidence level in auditing is almost totally dependent on the absolute size of the sample. It is practically independent of the total population or lot size from which the sample is taken. The sample size of the audit, therefore, should not be based on the lot size. And it should never be specified as a percent of the lot size! Strategic audits should use small sample sizes and be frequent enough to ensure that the information will be representative over time. More frequent audits with small sample sizes is a better approach than infrequent audits with large sample sizes.

It is a good idea to perform strategic audits on suppliers' shipments, but only enough to develop a "report card" on each supplier's performance and to measure the effectiveness of each supplier's prevention practices. For example, strategic audits might be used to track the process average defective rate of a supplier's production process. Strategic audits may also be used to generate information (notice I didn't say "data"!) on trends in vendor performance. Again, use small sample sizes with a planned periodic audit frequency. Since auditing is expensive, you only want to conduct just enough to obtain reasonable confidence on your performance and trend information. Any more auditing than that is a waste of time and money.

8

Breakthrough Improvement

Create innovative breakthrough
improvement for quality leadership
and superior market share.

IF IT AIN'T BROKE, FIX IT

The expression, "If it ain't broke, don't fix it," is now old, worn-out, and obsolete! If an organization is standing still and relying on yesterday's standards, then it is being overtaken and outdistanced by the competition. Those who want to rest on their laurels have already lost and just don't know it yet. Any past winner of the Indianapolis 500 race understands this instinctively.

Figure 8.1 shows cars in the 1955 and 2005 Indianapolis 500 races. Consider that in the 1955 Indianapolis 500 race, Bill Vukovich had the fastest lap with an average speed of 141.354 miles per hour. Fifty years later in the 2005 race, Tony Kanaan

1955 Indianapolis 500

2005 Indianapolis 500

IMS Photo

Figure 8.1 Yesterday's state-of-the-art is today's obsolescence.

had the fastest lap with an average speed of 228.102 miles per hour. Now, certainly there was nothing wrong with Bill Vukovich's car in 1955. It is quite clear, however, that without any innovation and improvement, his performance level soon becomes inadequate and obsolete.

Breakthrough improvement, in a sense, means constantly and deliberately "breaking it and fixing it." You must view yourself as your toughest competitor. You must constantly create new products that render your current products obsolete. This means you must fix it, even if it "ain't broke"—*especially* if it ain't broke. Any enterprise that doesn't understand this will end up trying to sell slide rules in a world of calculators (see Figure 8.2).

DRIVE BREAKTHROUGH IMPROVEMENT THROUGH CONTINUOUS INNOVATION

There is no such thing as product perfection, just as there is no such thing as product safety perfection. Although perfection may be a vision, it cannot be an achievable performance

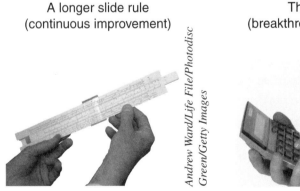

Figure 8.2   Beyond continuous improvement to breakthrough improvement.

standard. The performance standard, however, can and must be to achieve product excellence. Product excellence means that the product achieves the state-of-the-art performance standard with respect to consumer safety, quality, and technology. If you do not maintain an understanding of where the state of the art currently is and how to go about achieving it, consumer loyalty is vulnerable. That means your organization is vulnerable. To achieve consumer loyalty, a standard of product excellence must be achieved and maintained.

An organization that does not innovate will eventually die. Yesterday's standards do not hack it today, and today's standards will be inadequate tomorrow. To prevent organizational atrophy, it is mandatory to continually keep up with the constantly evolving technological environment. To ensure organizational vigor and success, it is important to keep pushing the leading edge of the state of the art. This requires more than just continuous improvement. It requires continuous innovation in search of radical, or breakthrough, improvement.

The following sections describe what can be done to ensure that your organization is in the right position for driving continuous innovation, breakthrough improvement, and product excellence.

BENEFIT FROM BENCHMARKING

It can be very beneficial to routinely meet with best-in-class, best-of-breed companies to search for new ideas, processes, methods, and best practices. This constant search for best practices must draw from a broad range of industries, since methods used in other industries can be valuable to your organization, often with very minimal modifications. Seeing what other industries are doing to build consumer loyalty and achieve competitive advantage can be very instructive.

The benchmarking activity involves touring the company's operation and sharing information to fully understand their systems, processes, and methodologies. This is especially important in the area of product safety and compliance. Sharing this type of information benefits not only both companies but also the consumer and, ultimately, society. It is important to your organization's success. It is also the right thing to do.

SERVE ON STANDARDS DEVELOPMENT COMMITTEES

Having representatives from your organization serve on standards development committees or industry association committees is important for understanding the state of the art with respect to industry standards. Even more beneficial is understanding the rationale behind each standard. This provides a special understanding and insight that ultimately ensures more thorough product design evaluations and better compliance.

Serving on these committees also provides the opportunity to participate in the standards development process to ensure that the discussions and considerations incorporate your organization's points of view. It allows your organization to constructively influence the content and rationale of new standards. This is especially important in the product safety area because it affords you the opportunity to prevent the promulgation of inadequate and incomplete standards that could otherwise unreasonably and unwittingly restrict your current and planned product lines.

Finally, serving on standards development committees provides an opportunity to network with representatives from other companies with a common interest. This can lead to excellent benchmarking activity.

CULTIVATE RELATIONSHIPS WITH REGULATORY BODIES

Maintaining a connectivity and rapport with regulatory agencies that have jurisdiction over your products can be very beneficial for your organization. It can help keep you ahead of regulatory changes, often even providing you with the opportunity to offer input and positive influence prior to the finalization of new and revised regulations. It can also give you firsthand knowledge as to how your products are tested, inspected, and evaluated.

Maintaining a communication link and positive relationship with compliance staff can give you special knowledge and insight into how compliance decisions are made. It can help keep you up to date on general injury data and patterns as well as contemplated and proposed standards. This can enable you to keep your internal safety standards advanced and relevant.

Building and maintaining a relationship with regulatory agency technical staff also provides valuable additional resources for your organization. They can provide very helpful guidance and direction to improve the thoroughness and effectiveness of the safety and quality evaluation of your new product concepts. These resources can sometimes become a significant economical extension of your own technical staff. Take advantage of their expertise where and when appropriate.

CONNECT WITH OUTSIDE TECHNICAL RESOURCES

It is generally not practical or financially feasible for an organization to have on hand all of the technical expertise necessary to thoroughly critique all new product innovations. There are just too many diverse technical areas. Some examples include expertise in chemistry, microbiology, physiology, acoustics, ophthalmology, psychology, toxicology, and human factors.

It is therefore necessary to expand your organizational competence with outside technical expertise by maintaining a network of technical experts to use as needed. This may include medical doctors or specialists at local hospitals, professors at local universities, outside professional laboratory personnel and experts, and, yes, even outside lawyers who specialize in product liability prevention. The point is that these experts really become an extension of your organization. They can be contacted when needed to provide evaluations, critiques, input, and direction. These connections can really help prevent an organization from falling into the "don't know what you don't know" danger zone shown in Figure 2.3.

EVALUATE YOUR COMPETITION

The primary focus of an organization must clearly be the consumer. It is all about delighting the consumer and continuing to earn their trust and loyalty. The consumer is king! However, a secondary focus must be your major competition. You must ensure that you are always staying ahead of your competition.

In the 1978 study by the Strategic Planning Institute, it was shown that product quality, *as perceived by the consumer relative to the competition*, is positively related to net profit and return on investment. Please refer back to Figures 3.1 and 3.2 for review.

It is therefore vitally important that your product be perceived by the consumer as superior to that of your general competition. To accomplish this, you must continually evaluate the product of your major competition against your own product. From time to time this may reveal weaknesses that must be corrected. This practice will help ensure that you keep ahead of your major competition.

KEEP A CLEAR AND SOUND
VISION AND STRATEGY

A sound vision and strategic plan are primary tools for leading an organization to sustainable growth and viability. A clear vision and plan promote teamwork and pull an organization in a common, positive direction that drives efficiency and effectiveness. To ensure that your vision and strategies are sound, you must be aware of the leading edge of the ever-changing state of the art. Benchmarking with best-in-class companies, serving on standards development committees, maintaining strong relationships with regulatory agencies, building a network of outside technical resources, and constantly evaluating the major competition will help provide that awareness. To do anything less is to let your organization and the consumer down.

9

Conclusion

Ostracize errors, variation, and
waste from your organization.

INSPIRE THE ORGANIZATION

Enabling excellence is really about having an inspired organization. It is about having an organization that comprehends what excellence is all about and how to apply relevant tools and concepts for achieving it. It is about having a culture of teamwork where errors, variation, and waste are constantly battled, and where mistakes and change are always embraced. It is about an environment where importance trumps urgency, where the focus is always on the vital few root causes, and where data is always converted into wisdom.

It is also about management priorities of brand building, continuous innovation, and constantly leading and pushing the state of the art in thought and technology. Most of all, it is about serving consumers to earn and keep their trust and loyalty.

When management concentrates on providing a clear and focused vision and plan and eliminating roadblocks and barriers to progress, it is macromanaging. Macromanagement inspires and motivates the organization and enables great teamwork to develop and thrive. It creates a challenging and fun environment where people are energized and motivated. This leads to higher levels of performance and achievement.

You now have the vision and plan for enabling excellence and for maintaining an inspired, high-performing organization. To accomplish this, all human resources must be focused on the seven vital elements:

1. Planning and preparing for error-free performance by eliminating the opportunities for error

2. Serving and delighting consumers, constantly working to protect them and to earn and keep their trust and loyalty

3. Verifying that processes are capable of meeting the requirements

4. Controlling the processes to prevent the production of errors/defects

5. Continually reducing variation, with the goal of zero variation

6. Applying the Pareto principle to identify the vital few causes, priorities, and opportunities

7. Driving continuous innovation and breakthrough improvement, constantly pushing the leading edge of state-of-the–art technology

These seven elements represent the key to enabling sustainable excellence and competitive advantage. They will also make your organization armed and dangerous to the "big three evils," and you will be inspired to ostracize them from your company.

OSTRACIZE THE THREE BIG EVILS

It is now time to take some urgent and important action. It is now time to:

- Eliminate delays in delivering product to your customer

- Eliminate material and product rejections during production

- Eliminate defective returns and complaints from your customers and consumers

- Eliminate product recalls, product liability lawsuits, and product safety concerns

In short, it is now time to ostracize errors, variation, and waste—the three big evils—from your organization.

Errors, variation, and waste are the big barriers to excellence. They must be eliminated. Enabling and empowering your organization to deal effectively with these three evils will allow it to begin achieving true excellence.

As errors, variation, and waste are prevented, excellence begins to grow. And this leads to building real consumer loyalty, substantial brand power, and strong competitive advantage. All of this will be made possible by the implementation of the seven vital foundational elements.

CREATE MASTERPIECES

Successful companies don't just create products, they create masterpieces. They think in terms of craftsmanship, social responsibility, and product integrity. They also think in terms of constant innovation, breakthrough improvement, and delighting the consumer. They constantly strive for higher levels of excellence.

These organizations are built on a solid foundation that enables excellence—a foundation of prevention, consumer focus, process capability, process control, reducing variation, applying the Pareto principle, and breakthrough improvement. They know how to build brand value and earn consumer trust and loyalty. They know how to create masterpieces. As a result, they enjoy a significant advantage over their competition.

Figure 9.1 shows some examples of masterpieces. The examples are diverse. Some are small and ingeniously simple. Others are large and relatively complex. However, they all share at least one characteristic: They provide consistently high value and delight to the consumer. The consumer has trust in them and is loyal to them. That is the sign of a true masterpiece.

ENABLE EXCELLENCE

You now have the basic ingredients for building a foundation for excellence in your company. You have the roadmap and

Figure 9.1 Examples of masterpieces.

basic tools for enabling excellence. Please remember that it is not about motivation, commitment, doing more, or working harder. It is about having the right plan and focusing on the vital few foundational concepts. Motivation, inspiration, enthusiasm, and commitment will be a result of enabling excellence, not a cause.

With the foundation for excellence in place, you can ostracize the three big evils and enable excellence to flourish in your organization. You can prepare your organization for creating masterpieces for your consumers and enjoying a real competitive advantage. Best wishes on your journey to excellence. Godspeed.

Appendix A

? ? Quiz ? ?

Ten Questions to Test Your Excellence Savvy

1. Safety Excellence

True or False

The most important reason safety goals are sometimes not achieved is an insufficient commitment to safety.

2. 100 Percent Inspection

True or False

The best way to achieve product excellence is to rely on 100 percent inspection.

3. Quality Standard

True or False

The quality standard must allow for some defects because everyone makes mistakes.

4. Root Causes of Errors

True or False

Lack of knowledge and lack of attention are the reasons for most errors/defects.

5. Schedule vs. Quality

True or False

It is better to get the job done on time with some defects than to be late with defect-free output.

6. Quality Measurement

True or False

The best measure of quality effectiveness is overall defective levels.

7. Industry Standards

True or False

The primary goal of a product safety function is to ensure that industry safety standards are met.

8. State of the Art

True or False

Manufacturers may be required to meet the state of the art with respect to product safety.

9. Conformance to Requirements

True or False

If the safety specification requires a product attachment to withstand 5 inch-pounds of torque, and 10 product attachments are tested to 5 inch-pounds of torque with no failure, then we have adequately demonstrated conformance to the safety requirement.

10. Cost vs. Quality

True or False

Higher quality means higher cost.

Please turn to Appendix B for the answers.

Appendix B

!! Answers !!

to the Quiz

1. Safety Excellence

False

Achieving product safety excellence is more about comprehension than commitment. It requires an understanding and application of prevention tools and processes, such as design hazard analysis, factors of safety, process capability analysis, and process control. People are generally very committed to product safety, but they are often unfamiliar with the right tools and how to apply them for achieving it.

REFERENCE: Chapter 1, "Comprehension vs. Commitment" section.

2. 100 Percent Inspection

False

100 percent inspection is not 100 percent effective. It is at best 80 percent effective. Depending on the type of product, type of defect, and inspection method, it can sometimes be less than 50 percent effective. In this case,

the majority of the defects will still remain after 100 percent inspection. The only way to achieve product excellence is to eliminate the opportunity for defects.

REFERENCE: Chapter 2, "Avoid Inspection" section.

3. Quality Standards

False

The quality standard must be zero defects. We must plan for and expect zero defects. The process that management provides to the worker must be capable of producing defect-free output. The goal, of course, is zero variation.

REFERENCE: Chapter 6, "Move from Zero Defects to Zero Variation" section.

4. Root Causes of Error

True

Lack of knowledge and lack of attention are the two root causes for most errors/defects.

REFERENCE: Chapter 2, "The Two Root Causes of Most Errors" section.

5. Schedule vs. Quality

False

It is always better to do the job right the first time than to do it over again later in the process. An effective prevention system ensures that quality is designed and built into the product, resulting in an on-time and defect-free output . . . consistently.

Note: A consumer who receives a defective product will not appreciate that it was delivered on time!

REFERENCE: Chapter 3, "High Quality Means High Profitability" section.

6. Quality Measurement

False

Defective rates are good indicators, but the best measure of quality effectiveness is reduced total quality costs, especially failure costs.

REFERENCE: Chapter 2, "The Prevention Concept" section.

7. Industry Standards

False

Industry standards may not cover every possible product safety consideration. In a study of U.S. Consumer Product Safety Commission recall information, approximately 80 percent of the recalled product met all mandatory and industry standards. Although it is important and necessary to meet industry standards, it is often not sufficient.

The primary goal of a product safety function is to protect the consumer against unreasonable risks of injury. An awareness and understanding of consumer injury data and reasonably foreseeable consumer use and misuse are very important factors that must be included in a comprehensive product safety system.

REFERENCE: Chapter 3, "Build Brands, Not Commodities" section.

8. State of the Art

True

Product safety perfection is not possible or expected. Product safety excellence, however, is achieved when the state of the art is achieved in standards and technology.

REFERENCE: Chapter 1, "State of the Art vs. Perfection" section.

9. Conformance to Requirements

False

If 10 units are tested to the specification and all pass, the best you can state is that you are 90 percent confident that the true failure rate is less than about 20 percent (refer to Figure 4.1 in Chapter 4). This result is not acceptable for product safety. The correct procedure is to test to failure and calculate the test failure average and standard deviation. From these two parameters (average and standard deviation) the failure rate in parts per million defective can be determined.

REFERENCE: Chapter 4, "Test to Failure, Not to Specification" section.

10. Cost vs. Quality

False

Since quality is defined as "conformance to requirements" (in other words, freedom from defects), then higher quality results in lower costs—less repair, scrap, customer and consumer returns, and so forth. Remember, the best organizations spend the *least* on quality.

REFERENCES: Chapter 2, "The Prevention Concept" section; Chapter 3, "High Quality Means High Profitability" section.

Index